Consequences of DIVORCE

Consequences of DIVORCE

Barbara White Hege

Inscript

Bladensburg, MD

Consequences of Divorce

**Published by
Dove Christian Publishers
P.O. Box 611
Bladensburg, MD 20710-0611
www.dovechristianpublishers.com**

Copyright © 2019 by BARBARA WHITE HEGE

Cover Design by Mark Yearnings

All rights reserved. No part of this publication may be used or reproduced without permission of the publisher, except for brief quotes for scholarly use, reviews or articles.

Scriptures quotations marked KJV are from the King James Version of the Bible (public domain).

ISBN: 9781732112568

Printed in the United States of America

Dedication

In memory of my Mother, Emily Dockery White Jenkins and my brother, Billy Lee White.

Contents

Dedication v
Chapter 1 1
Chapter 2 3
Chapter 3 5
Chapter 4 7
Chapter 5 9
Chapter 6 11
Chapter 7 13
Chapter 8 15
Chapter 9 17
Chapter 10 19
Chapter 11 21
Chapter 12 23
Chapter 13 25
Chapter 14 27
Chapter 15 29
Chapter 16 31
Chapter 17 33
Chapter 18 35
Chapter 19 36
Chapter 20 37
Chapter 21 38
Chapter 22 40
Chapter 23 41
Chapter 24 43
Chapter 25 45
Chapter 26 47
Chapter 27 48
Chapter 28 52
Chapter 29 54

Chapter 1

"Emily, I saw Adam and Ruth together up at West End." This was Daddy's sister, Mattie Mae, talking to my mother. I think I was five or six years old when I heard those words. My brother, Bill, was two or three years old. Little did I know how those words and what they revealed would affect the rest of my life. I remember exactly where we were when Mattie Mae uttered them. I don't think it could be so, but it seems I understood what those words meant, even at that young age.

Daddy and Mother ran a little country grocery store/service station a few miles from Elkin, North Carolina, which was owned by my paternal grandfather and was located next door to where he and my grandmother lived. This was one of those stores where people didn't just come in to buy something. They often sat, drank sodas, and visited together. I remember my maternal grandmother telling my Mother to watch Ruth, that she was after my daddy. She stated she had seen her flirting with him. Ruth lived just down the road from the store and was in and out sometimes. My Daddy was not a Christian then and had an eye for the ladies. So started an affair that would go on for eleven years or more.

During those eleven years, Daddy left twice, returning home each time after a few months. He had broken off the affair a couple of times and somehow allowed himself to be lured back into it. I was told that at least one of those times, Ruth threatened suicide. About five or six years into the affair, she became pregnant, giving birth to a daughter, Vickie, in March 1950. I was in the seventh grade. That year at Christmas, Daddy bought Christmas presents for me, Mother, and Bill. This was the first and only time he ever did this by himself. I received a new gold watch. Bill received a new bicycle. Mother received a new gold wedding band. Looking back on this years later, I believe this came from the guilt he must have been feeling.

The second time he left, he ended up in the hospital with a nervous breakdown and was placed in the psychiatric ward. Vickie was around two years old at the time. I think I was thirteen years old, and Bill was ten. He sent someone to ask if Bill and I would come to visit him. He asked for Mother to visit with us, also. We discovered that he and Ruth were living together in a small town about two hours away. We did honor his request and visited him in the hospital there. After being there for some time, he was released by his doctors and came back home. He left for the third time when I was a senior in high school. He never returned.

Chapter 2

Let's go back for a minute. When I was seven or eight years old, Daddy and Mother bought a large farm. We were living there when Daddy left. Each time he left, he would just disappear. Mother, Bill, and I would be visiting a neighbor or my grandparents, only to return home and discover that Daddy had packed his clothes and left. We had no idea where he was living. I don't know how we made it during those times, because we were always left with no money. However, somehow God made a way. I don't remember our ever wanting for anything. Moreover, after his leaving, Mother rented the farmland, so we eventually had income from that.

As Bill and I were so young when all this started, we grew up under the scandal of this affair. Such sins may be viewed differently today by the world. But not by God, who still declares it sin. Hebrews 13:8 tells us He is the same yesterday, today and tomorrow. He does not change. His Word does not change. Psalm 119:89 says, "Forever, oh Lord, thy Word is settled in heaven" (KJV).

It seemed everyone knew about the affair. Mother was so well-liked and respected that it was not as much a reflection on her or us as it was on Daddy and Ruth. In spite of this, Daddy was well-liked also.

Mother was, in my opinion, a saint through all of this. I

always wondered why she stayed with Daddy all those years. Maybe it was because she had nowhere to go with two small kids. Or perhaps she still loved him? It may have been because divorce is a sin and not an option (Malachi 2:16 "For the Lord, the God of Israel, says He hates putting away..."). I remember hearing divorce discussed many times during those years and what the Bible taught about it. However, regardless of why she stayed, it was amazing how she treated my Dad during this time. Sometimes Daddy would rant and rave over some insignificant thing (Looking back, I think he sometimes took all the frustrations of his sin out on her). Mother would just let him vent until he ran out of words. And in spite of everything, she was always good to him. How she did this, with all that was going on, had to be only by the grace of God.

Chapter 3

As for me, I was able to compartmentalize this, to some extent, and go forward with my life–making the best of a difficult situation. I don't mean to minimize the trauma of this. It was painful. But somehow, God gave me the ability to prevent it from dominating my life. Even though there was some shame, God's protection was there even in that. It seemed to be more Daddy and Ruth's shame than mine. I don't remember ever feeling as if I were less because of it, although my brother did experience some personal reactions from it. When he was in high school, a schoolmate would not associate with him because of this. This schoolmate then tried to turn others against Bill and get them to be his friend rather than Bill's. Actually, I think part of this may have been jealousy on the guy's part because Bill was outgoing, tall, dark, and handsome.

I was very active throughout school. I had lead roles in school programs and plays in elementary school. In high school, I served as the class president, vice-president, and reporter; was the chief cheerleader and the school and county spelling champion; and placed second in the state championship. I was the co-editor of our yearbook, had a leading role in the junior year play and a smaller role in the senior play. I was involved in other things too numerous to mention. I graduated at the top of my class, receiving the honor of valedictorian. And Daddy missed all of this. Even when he was home, he gave no attention to things I was involved in at school. When I made my valedictory speech on class night, and when I graduated the next day, I did not even know where Daddy was. As usual, he had left home without telling us anything. A few years later, he missed my wedding. I still did not know where he was living. I thank God for my involvement in all these activities. Even though I didn't realize it at the time, I believe God used this busy-ness to help carry me through all those years.

I remember the first time I realized some of what I was missing in a father. I had gone home with a friend from school and saw the relationship between her and her daddy. I realized that Daddy and I did not have that kind of relationship, and it made me a little envious and sad. He was my Daddy, and I loved him, but the relationship was definitely lacking.

I learned at an early age not to allow my mind to dwell on things I could do nothing to change and to go on and make the best of it. Although the Bible gives us instructions on this, I was not aware of them at that time. Nonetheless, I believe God was working the principle of Philippians 4:8 in me: "Finally, brethren, whatever things are true, whatever things are honest, whatever things are just, whatever things are pure, whatever things are of good report; if there be any virtue, if there be any praise, think on these things." I still have to do that sometimes. I ask God to help me turn my mind from things that hurt, offend, and cause anger; and to think on those things listed in Philippians, on Him, and the many blessings He has given me. I remember the scripture in Isaiah 26:3, "Thou will keep him in perfect peace whose mind is stayed on thee, because he trusts in you."

Chapter 4

Since Bill and I were older when Daddy left home permanently in 1955, I am thankful we never experienced having to spend every other weekend with the 'other parent.' I am positive neither of us would have been happy with this situation, as some today are not. I have a family member who struggles today with a similar arrangement. She has a friend in school who struggles with the same situation. Perhaps it does not bother some children. I do not know. I suppose it depends on the relationship with the 'every other weekend' parent. But sometimes the child is unhappy about having the family life disrupted and having to leave home every other weekend. I can certainly understand that.

There seems to be no good answer for this when divorce happens. But, again, sin has consequences for both the parents and the innocent children involved. Please understand, I did not label it as sin. God did. The Bible says in Matthew 19:6, "what God has therefore joined together, let no man put asunder." And yes, God forgives this sin when there is confession and repentance just as He forgives any other sin, but, like any sin, there are still consequences, and sometimes they are lifelong.

David was said to be a man after God's own heart. Yet, he suffered the consequences of sin in his life. He had taken Bathsheba and lay with her. When he learned she had conceived, he conspired to have her husband killed in battle. In 2 Samuel 12:10, God sent Nathan with this message to David: "Why have you despised the commandment of the Lord, to do evil in His sight? You have killed Uriah, the Hittite, with the sword and have taken his wife to be thy wife and has slain him with the sword of the children of Ammon. Now, therefore, the sword shall never depart from your house, because you have despised me, and have taken the wife of Uriah, the Hittite to be your wife." If you continue reading 2 Samuel, you will see that David was forgiven, but he still suffered the consequences of his sin. He was told the baby Bathsheba was carrying would die. One of his sons raped his half-sister. And the list goes on.

We are also told in Hebrews 12:6 that God chastises those whom He loves. Sin always has consequences.

Chapter 5

After graduation in 1955, I moved to Winston-Salem, North Carolina and went to work in the office of what was then Western Electric (now AT&T). I was barely seventeen years old (graduated a year early, having skipped second grade). Around three years after moving there, I was scheduled to go on a date with Bob Porterfield. However, a friend wanted me to go on a blind date with another Bob. I told her no, and that I already had a date for that night. She persisted and finally talked me into breaking the date with Bob Porterfield and accepting this blind date. After going to a movie that evening, we went to Staley's Restaurant, which was the hangout at that time. Kids parked on the curb, ordered, and visited. Several of my date's friends were there also and were parked on the curb. If you can believe more Bobs, they were Bob Barney, Bob Hege, and Bill Bailey. I was introduced to them, never dreaming that one of them would eventually become my husband.

As God would have it, I would cross paths with Bob Hege occasionally after that. We would talk briefly and probably flirt a bit. He eventually called my job (he didn't have my home phone number at that time) asking for a date. I accepted, and so began our relationship that has lasted sixty-plus years. We dated three months and were married on November 22, 1958. Marrying this quickly isn't something I recommend, but it has worked for Bob and me.

I'm not usually easily persuaded, which is why I sometimes wonder why I allowed myself to be talked into breaking a date with someone whom I respected and going on this blind date. I had gone on one blind date in high school and had vowed I would never do that again. Later, I came to realize this was God's work in bringing Bob and me together. (As of this writing, we celebrated our 60th wedding anniversary). God has blessed us with a daughter, Lisa, who was born in January 1963. She and her husband, Ken Neaves, were married on our 30th wedding anniversary and live about ten minutes from us. We have two granddaughters, Rachel and Anna; and one great-granddaughter, Riley. I like to say they have the right name—grand! I love all of them so much.

Chapter 6

Several years after leaving home, Daddy came back to see us and to tell us where he was living. He was living in Mims/Titusville, Florida and was working at Cape Canaveral. We remained in contact until he came back to North Carolina to live. He came back with Ruth and their daughter, Vickie. He and Ruth were now married. They lived two miles from my mother and my brother. I cannot speak for Mother in this, but it was not easy for me. When I went home to visit Mother, I would not go out there to visit Daddy and Ruth at all. To do so would make me feel disloyal to Mother, although she never said or did anything to make me feel that way. But I was also harboring unforgiveness in my heart. And God began dealing with me on this.

Every time we would go to Mom's, I would be convicted of my unforgiving spirit. I finally relented—knowing that if Daddy died, I did not want to look at him and realize I had treated him badly. I did not want to keep disobeying God by a lack of forgiveness. Colossians 3:13 says, "Forbearing one another, and forgiving one another; if any man have a quarrel against any: even as Christ forgave you, so also do ye." I am often reminded of how much God has forgiven me and how we, as His forgiven children, should forgive others with thanksgiving to God in Christ Jesus.

In forgiving and visiting Daddy and Ruth, I struggled with

feelings of disloyalty to Mother. I knew I was not disloyal in forgiving, but it was the way I felt. But God has taught me that we do not necessarily live or make decisions by our feelings, but by His Word. Feelings sometimes come and go. Feelings often change. They are not always reliable, and they can lead us astray. So, I did what I knew God wanted me to do, although the feelings persisted from time to time. I had to ignore those feelings and choose to obey God. So much of our Christian walk is a choice. We make choices on whether to obey or disobey God. When we choose to obey Him, He has given us the Holy Spirit to enable us to do this. We are never left to our own resources. Psalm 46:1 says, "God is our refuge and strength; a very present help in trouble."

Chapter 7

We are commanded to forgive others. In doing this, I learned we cannot allow our mind to dwell on the wrongs that have been committed. If we do, old feelings will often surface, feelings of resentment, anger, etc. So, we look to God to help us put those things aside; to help us turn our mind from wrongs committed against us. His Word helps us. We ask the Holy Spirit to help us think on the things listed in the scripture from Philippians 4:8-9 that I mentioned earlier. We ask Him to enable us to be obedient to Colossians 3:12-14 and to "Put on, therefore, as the elect of God, holy and beloved, tender mercies, kindness, humbleness of mind, meekness, longsuffering; forbearing one another, and forgiving one another; if any man have a quarrel against any, even as Christ forgave you, so also do you. And above all these things, put on love, which is the bond of perfectness."

Matthew 5:44 says: "But I say unto you, Love your enemies, bless them that curse you, do good to them that hate you, and pray for them which despitefully use you, and persecute you." This sounds impossible, doesn't it? But it can be done when, by an act of our will, we submit to God in making the decision to obey Him. The Holy Spirit enables us to do what is impossible to do on our own. I've also learned when I pray for someone who mistreats me,

God honors that and, despite their actions, He enables me to care for them as human beings created by Him.

Chapter 8

On my own, I would have been like a lot of families I see today who have broken relationships. They do not speak to one another for years, being filled with anger, resentment, and unforgiveness. Then one dies, and the ones left are often filled with regret. Their disobedience to God comes back to haunt them. Ephesians 4:31-32 tells us, "Let all bitterness, wrath, anger, clamor, and evil speaking be put away from you with all malice. And be kind to one another, tenderhearted, forgiving one another, even as God, for Christ's sake, has forgiven you" (NKJV).

But, for the grace of God, I could have continued in my unforgiving spirit, having nothing to do with Daddy and Ruth. In doing so, I would have made life so much more difficult on myself and others involved. In Acts 9:5, we are warned about this. Paul was persecuting the church and was on the road to Damascus when Jesus spoke to him, saying, "I am Jesus, whom you are persecuting. It is hard for you to kick against the goads." This seems to say that by refusing to accept a situation we cannot change and fighting against it, we are making it harder on ourselves. This is so true. Acceptance of a situation we cannot change ends the battle, and we cease to struggle or fight against it. Then we can move on with our lives, trusting in God, and doing the best we can in a perhaps difficult situation. Again, I was not aware of nor did I understand this scripture, but God was working it in me.

To clarify, accepting a situation that cannot be changed does not always mean we endorse it or become a part of it. Sin is rampant in this world. We, as Christians, accept the fact that everyone has the 'right' to live as they please. God gives them/us that 'right,' although "He is long-suffering toward us, not willing that any should perish, but that all would come to repentance." But, giving one that right does not mean God endorses or condones sin. He does not. So, we do not endorse it or become a part of it. We continue to stand against it, standing with and on God's Word. Second Thessalonians 3:6,14 reads, "Now we command you, brethren, in the name of our Lord Jesus Christ, that ye withdraw yourselves from every brother that walketh disorderly, and not after the tradition which he received of us.... And if any man obey not our word by this epistle, note that man, and have no company with him, that he may be ashamed." But He is always is willing to forgive our sin when we put our faith in Jesus Christ and repent.

Chapter 9

Even though Daddy and Ruth lived so close to Mother, I did not visit them every time I went home. This was not because of a lack of forgiveness. It was from the difference in the relationship, plus it limited the amount of time I could spend with Mother. But I still began to feel guilty about that. It was especially difficult during the holidays, in trying to work out time to spend with Bob's family, with Mother and my family, and with Daddy's. But, as I prayed about it, God gave me peace with it. He made me realize that this was Daddy's choice; that he had left us, and this was what he chose. He chose a life apart from us, and I did not have to divide the time equally between him and Mother. Even though I no longer felt the need to make it equal, it still was not easy. I did not want to hurt Daddy's feelings, but, again, I was reminded that he had to live with the consequences of his sin (his choice) just as we did. I'm not sure this can be expressed enough: sin has consequences, not just for the person committing it, but also for those close to the person. A quote by Ravi Zacharias reads, "Sin will take you farther than you want to go, keep you longer than you want to stay, and cost you more than you want to pay." This is so very true.

But even in forgiving, there was much to contend with, such as realizing I didn't really like Ruth all that well. Because of this, I began to question if I had really forgiven her. But, again, in praying to God, He made me realize that even if Ruth had never known my Daddy, I still would not really like her all that much because of her personality. In life, we meet people we really like, and some we don't really like that much. We cannot make ourselves love someone emotionally, but we can love them with agape love through the power of the Holy Spirit. He enabled me to love Ruth through my actions, but because of her personality, I could not really make myself *like* her. Now, I could tell you the things in her personality that kept me from really liking her, but my purpose in writing this is not to 'smear' another person, which is another function of the agape love I have for her.

Chapter 10

I knew nothing about agape love at the time, although I believe God was working it in and through me. I was simply accepting a situation I could do nothing to change and making the best of it. To do that, I had to accept that Ruth was now Daddy's wife and a part of the family. And to make the best of this situation, I needed to forgive her (and Daddy), be nice to her, and treat her well, despite my feelings. That's really what agape love is—not necessarily a feeling or emotion, but an act of our will. We decide to obey God and to love someone in this way—through our actions—and God gives us the ability to do so because it is pleasing to Him.

When the Bible tells us in Matthew 5:44 to "love your enemies, bless them that curse you, do good to them that hate you, and pray for them which despitefully use you, and persecute you," He isn't talking about emotional love. We can't make ourselves love someone that way. He is speaking of agape love. By an act of our will in obedience to Him, we decide to agape love them by our actions. As we yield ourselves and our will to Him and His will, the Holy Spirit enables us to obey Him in this way. Even then, it is not always easy. But I do not see where God has always promised to make something easy, but He does make it possible. You see, it is never all about us, but about Him as

He works in and through us. I did not understand all this at the time, but God did, and He was working it in me.

Chapter 11

In our walk with God, we are sometimes called to give up what we want, or to ignore our feelings. We may not 'feel' like forgiving someone or treating them well. But we choose to ignore our feelings and make our decisions based on God's Word—the right thing to do. We are much happier people when we do this and walk in fellowship with Him. God knows this and always wants the best for those of us who are His children.

Isaiah 48:18 reads, "Oh, that thou hadst hearkened to my commandments! Then had thy peace been like a river, and thy righteousness like the waves of the sea."

In writing this and praying about how to explain ignoring our feelings, I realized it is the giving of one's self sacrificially to obey God. We are told in Romans 12:1, "I beseech you, therefore, brethren, by the mercies of God, that ye present your bodies, a living sacrifice, holy, acceptable unto God, which is your reasonable service." Sacrifice often means giving up what we want. We do this to be obedient to Him and His Word; yielding our heart, mind, body, and spirit to Him, to serve Him in whatever way He chooses; allowing Him to be Lord of our lives. There is great reward in this. From a human perspective, it may not sound rewarding, but with submission to Him and His will comes that "perfect peace that passes all understanding" as stated in Philippians

4:7. There is no greater joy than the joy of being in fellowship with Him.

Jesus sacrificed greatly to give us salvation, the forgiveness of our sins, and a new life with and in Him. We can never know how much He sacrificed. But we know He gave up for thirty-three years (at least to some extent) the glory He shared with the Father. He gave thirty-three years to walk among the evil in this world and among sinners, remaining holy and sinless in spite of all this. We cannot even imagine the suffering he bore on the cross, not only from the painful, cruel death but also the bearing of our sins. Isaiah 52:14 says, "As many were astonied at thee; his visage was so marred more than any man, and his form more than the sons of men." How can we not freely give ourselves to one Who loves us so much?

Chapter 12

I want to once again make it clear that loving (agape love) Ruth, even in my actions, came only through the grace of God and the power of His Holy Spirit. He gave me the grace to be nice to her and treat her well all those years. I could never have done it on my own, and even then, sometimes it wasn't easy. But it was a real lesson in His grace being sufficient. Second Corinthians 12:9 reads, "And He said to me, 'My grace is sufficient for you, for My strength is made perfect in weakness.'"

Notice the scripture mentioned earlier in Matthew 5:44. It does not say to feel something. It says to *do* something. It says "Bless them" — again being obedient to God and the Holy Spirit will enable. It says, "do good" to them in spite of their actions. It says, "pray for them." Choose to do this in obedience to God. We are not held accountable by God for how other people treat us, but we are held responsible for how we treat them.

You know God extends His grace to us through Jesus Christ; His death, burial, and resurrection, forgiving us our sins even though we don't deserve it. He does not like our sin; He hates sin. But His grace is given to us anyway when we come to know Jesus as our Savior and Lord. We may not like something someone does to us. We never will if what they have done or are doing is wrong. But we are called to extend grace to them who, like us, often do not deserve it.

Chapter 13

When Vickie became engaged to James Calhoun and was planning her wedding, she asked me to be her Matron of Honor. I did not really want to do this because of so much that had gone before. I knew some people apparently thought I should have nothing to do with Daddy and Ruth. And I could just imagine the criticism I might get in agreeing to do this. I struggled with this decision. I was in a place or position I didn't really want to be in. I knew what people thought shouldn't have made any difference, especially when their thinking was wrong, and when I wasn't doing anything to displease God. There again came the realization that we do not live by feelings, but by the will of our Lord. I did not want to hurt Vickie, so I agreed. Even so, this was not easy for me to do, but by the grace of God, it was made possible. He is sufficient for our every need. He was and is teaching me to put self aside to serve Him and others, and to be obedient to Him as much as possible in all things. Am I perfect at this? No, not by a long shot. But God is patient and continues to work in and on me.

In March 1987, Vickie was killed in a drive-by shooting. A young girl and two young men were driving in the neighborhood, and one young man was firing into windows of homes where the lights were on. Vickie was standing in the living room of her home talking to her husband, J.C. when the bullet came through the window, killing her instantly. She crumpled to the floor in front of him.

I was spending the night with Mother when Bob called me. J.C. had called our home to ask us to go and tell this awful news to Daddy and Ruth. Since I was at Mother's and in the area, delivering this message fell to me. This was very difficult to do. During this time, God reminded me He knew all about our grief, for He had watched His Son die on a cross. As He died, He prayed for those who were killing Him, saying, "Father, forgive them...." And in that brief moment, I knew the attitude God wanted us to have in this situation.

Chapter 14

In the following days, I found myself again in a situation I did not want to be in. It was as if I put all my emotions on hold. Her husband, J.C., sobbed through almost the entire funeral, and I did not shed a tear during this entire time. This is almost unheard of, since I cry very easily. It was not that I did not care, and I really cannot explain it. It was almost like I was on autopilot. I walked through this time only through the strength of the Lord Who has never failed me.

The newspaper contacted Daddy, then called me. I could see God's hand in even this. Neither Daddy nor I knew what the other said at this point. Yet our answers were similar.

This was Daddy's response to them and what they printed:

"I just want these people brought to justice. I am not trying to be vengeful; I do not feel that. The Lord says, 'Vengeance is mine.' There is nothing we can do to help Vickie. It seems her death is something unreal."

My response was:

"I guess our feelings are that we are glad they are caught — not because we want revenge, but because we do not want another family to perhaps suffer in this way. We are Christians, and I know that God forgives us if we repent. Our prayers are that they (the alleged assailants) will come to know the Lord; that the young men and woman come to know Jesus in a personal

way."

The newspaper also stated the following: "Hege also had prayers for the families of the killers. She stated: 'I have a 24-year-old daughter, and my heart would be breaking if she did something like this.'"

Chapter 15

In November, a few weeks before Thanksgiving, came the trial of the young girl who was driving the car on that fateful night. During this time, I sat in that courtroom and marveled silently at the work God had done in me because I could not really hate her. Oh, I hated what she had done, but I could feel no real hatred for her. I could remember a time when that is all I would have felt. This does not mean I was never tempted—I was tempted often. At one point, I was so angry at what was happening in the courtroom, that I actually sat there and debated whether to risk contempt of court. But I was never left in that anger because I have an advocate with the Father, Jesus Christ. Each time, He would take the anger and turn it into a prayer—first, for myself, and then for the recipient of that anger. Now, I did not pray for her to go free because I believe we must be held responsible for our actions. But I did pray that she and the others involved would turn to Jesus.

How could I do this? How could I pray for someone who had done this to my family?

Well, there were many reasons, and I will give you two. First, God made me so aware that He died for her just as He died for me. John 3:16 says, "For God so loved the world that He gave His only begotten Son, that whosoever believes in Him should not perish, but have everlasting life." And, I knew that she was included in that 'whosoever.' Secondly, I could not do it because of any good in me. On my own, I am neither that good nor that forgiving. But, I could do it, because that's the difference Jesus Christ makes.

The trial ended the day before Thanksgiving. As you can imagine, feelings/emotions ran high. It lasted three and one-half stressful weeks. When the jury came back from their deliberations, she was convicted of first-degree murder. As this happened, tears rolled down my cheeks. Those tears were a release of emotions. They were for the loss of Vickie; for the family; and yes, for a twenty-six-year-old girl (only one year older than my own daughter) whom I saw ruining her life for the 'pleasures of sin.' You may question again how I could do this and how I could shed one tear for someone who had done this to Vickie and to our family. I will tell you I could do it only through the power of the Holy Spirit within me. I could do it through our God who tells us in 2 Peter 3:9 that He "…is long suffering towards us, not willing that any should perish, but that all should come to repentance" (NKJV).

Before the end of the trial, the Lord gave me the opportunity to witness to her and the third young man who was in the car. He had apparently passed out in the back seat of the car and was not awake when the shooting occurred. I don't know if any of them ever came to know the Lord.

Somehow, I never had the opportunity to witness to the person who actually fired the shot, but I did pray for him.

Chapter 16

During the trial of the actual shooter, I could see it taking a toll on us. It was much more stressful than the trial of the young girl who was driving the car. It lasted three weeks. But I found God to be just as sufficient as before. I've learned that God does not always change my situations so much as He changes me and my attitude in them.

I also remember having some misgivings about some of the jurors that were being selected. I was not thrilled with some that were chosen and the answers they gave. I was Chairman of Christian Women's Club at the time, and I called our board requesting prayer for this. As it turned out, after three weeks of testimony, we ended up with a hung jury. And it was declared a mistrial. We discovered later that two of the jurors stated they would not vote 'guilty' regardless of any evidence shown.

I wondered why. But I have learned to trust God with my 'whys' and to trust in Him with all my heart. I often hold on to Proverbs 3:5, "Trust in the Lord with all your heart and lean not on your own understanding" (NKJV). I can honestly tell you this makes all the difference in the world to me, just learning to trust Him even when I don't understand why, and regardless of the circumstances.

Thanks to a determined Assistant District Attorney, there was a second trial for the alleged shooter. It was moved to another court district. A few days into the trial, I could see the jury had made up their mind about the guilt of the perpetrated shooter. I do not remember the length of this trial, but once the testimony was over, the jury's deliberation began, and it was swift. When we heard they had reached a verdict, one of the detectives on the case said to me, "This is not good. This verdict was reached too quickly." For just a moment, I felt a little panicky. But then I said, "No, they made up their mind on this early in the trial." The young man was found guilty of first-degree murder and received a life sentence.

During the trial, as I looked at the person responsible for Vickie's death, again I could remember a time when I would have been so blinded by anger and hatred (I think perhaps *rage* would not be too strong a word), that all I would have seen would have been a murderer. I cannot tell you that I did not still see that. But because of Jesus Christ, I saw something else. I saw a young man who needed to know the Lord Jesus Christ. He may have taken someone from us that we loved, and he had no right to do that. He may have caused us tremendous grief and pain, and he had no right to do that. But his sin was against God, and I knew he would someday ultimately answer to the Lord. And, if God has forgiven me all my sin (and He has), who am I not to forgive another person?

Chapter 17

Also, during this third trial, we learned that the bullet that killed Vickie shattered into three parts as it went through the picture window. The large part of the bullet went into the wall. Only a sliver of the bullet hit Vickie's heart. As this information came out, it seemed as if God were saying to me, "This is from me."

In relation to that, on June 24, 1987, three months after Vickie's death, I was reading in Isaiah 40:21-22: "Have you not known? Have you not heard? Has it not been told you from the beginning? Have you not understood from the foundation of the earth? It is He Who sits above the circle of the earth, and the inhabitants are like grasshoppers; Who stretches out the heavens like a curtain; and spreads them like a tent to dwell in" (RSV). As I was reading this, the Holy Spirit lifted my heart to Him in praise of Who He is. Then in verse 24, the theme of the scripture changed, saying "Yea, they shall not be planted; yea, they shall not be sown; yea, their stock shall not take root in the earth; and he shall also blow upon them, and they shall wither, and the whirlwind shall take them away like stubble."

In reading this verse, the Holy Spirit spoke (not literally but to my spirit) making this scripture so real to me. It was as if God were saying the seed of Daddy and Ruth would not be planted, would not be sown, nor take root in the earth. Then

I understood why Vickie and J.C. had not had any children. Also, I felt He was speaking of Daddy and Ruth in saying, "they shall wither." Both had always been very slim but become so much thinner during their last days.

Chapter 18

Sometime after moving back to North Carolina, Daddy and Ruth made a profession of faith in Jesus Christ and were baptized. Sometime after this, with tears running down his cheeks, Daddy apologized to us more than once for what he had done. He told us if he could do it over, things would be different. But that is the thing about sin. There are no do-overs. There is forgiveness, yes, if we confess and repent, but no do-overs. Through the power of the Holy Spirit living within us, however, we can make each new day better.

Ruth sat and listened to him do this each time, but never once said she was sorry. I know some of you are wondering how my brother and I could forgive her under these circumstances. Again, it was only through the grace of God and the power of the Holy Spirit. God will do in and through us what we cannot do on our own if we are submitted to Him and willing to be obedient. The Bible says that God commends His love to us in that, while we were yet sinners, Christ died for us. He commands us to forgive others, just as He, for Christ's sake, has forgiven us. So, Bill and I chose to obey and passed on to Ruth a bit of the same grace given to us.

Chapter 19

I'm not absolutely sure Daddy ever forgave himself for what he did. He would bring it up from time to time when we were alone. He was in the hospital in January before he died in May. I stayed with him during this time, and he brought it up again, saying how sorry he was. I would tell him, "Daddy, you can't go back and undo what has happened. You've got to stop beating yourself up over something that can't be changed and accept the fact that you are forgiven. It's in the past, and we need to leave it there, thanking God for love and forgiveness in Jesus Christ."

I think, hope, that perhaps he was finally able to do that. I was with him when he died in the hospital in May 2004, and he had not brought it up again.

When he died, I grieved and cried for the loss. I also cried for all that he missed. My crying and grief for all Bill and I had missed in a Dad were in the past. So I cried for the loss of him and for all he missed. And I often thought that all we missed in a Dad, God made up for, as much as possible, in our Mother. I will tell more about Mother later.

Chapter 20

As I stated earlier, he missed so much of my and Bill's life. He missed being the Dad his son needed so much. He missed being the Dad for me and having the relationship I wish we could have had in those earlier years, although God did give us a good relationship in later years. He missed our family times together (cookouts, picnics in the mountains, holidays together). He would have loved those. Even though we did spend time with him, it was not the same as when all the family was together. And, somewhere along the way, God helps us to understand that the ground at the foot of the cross is level. None of us are higher or better than the other. All of us make mistakes. All of us have and will sin. So, we go forward with what we have—forgiveness and God, Who loves us.

So much sadness, but we cannot dwell there. We must dwell on all we have to be thankful for and give God the glory and honor due to His Name. I know God placed me in the family He wanted me to have. He gave me the parents He wanted me to have and gave me to them. I love all of them. He placed me there for a purpose. Sometimes I think I have an idea of why, but I am not sure. And what really matters is that His will be done, and whatever the purpose was or is, I pray that it was and is being fulfilled.

Chapter 21

I was 66 years old when Daddy died, and 68 when Ruth died, so you can see this covered a large portion of my life. Before Daddy died, he wanted to give me their power-of-attorney, which they did. I felt Ruth didn't really want to do that, and also that she did not want Daddy to know that. Apparently, that was true because shortly after his death, she took away the power-of-attorney and gave it to her niece. She did not tell me she was doing this. The attorney informed me about it. I had a feeling that she had also changed her will at that time; and, of course, we found out after she died that she had indeed changed it. This was against what she had agreed to with Daddy — that whatever money and property were left after the last one's death would be left to Billy and me.

My first thoughts when I read her new will was that I could not believe anyone would do this. It was especially unbelievable that she would give to her nieces the house, money, CDs, and stock that had been willed to Daddy by his daddy and our granddaddy. I also could not believe that her nieces would take it, knowing it should come to Bill and me.

The amount the nieces received, including the car, was (the best I could determine) around $400,000, divided among the four of them. It could have been more (in fact, I had been told there was more), but this is what I knew from stock,

CDs, sale of the house, etc. Bill and I received a little less than 20,000 dollars each. There were some other bequests (some left intact from the prior wills) to the church, to J.C. Calhoun, Vickie's husband; a fund set up for flowers; some to the grandchildren (some of whom offered theirs to Bill and me, which we would not accept). The filing of the will settlement at the courthouse was not correct. For instance, they listed the house as selling for $150,000. I called a friend at the courthouse and learned that it actually sold for $250,000.

Chapter 22

Since I also believe God is in control and nothing can touch me, except He either wills or allows it, I could not understand why He would allow this to happen to Bill and me after all that had gone before for so many years. So, God took me to that verse I "hang on" to so often: "Trust in the Lord with all your heart and lean not to your own understanding." When I don't understand, there's one thing I can do—I can trust in Him with all my heart. Again, this made all the difference in the world—just trusting in Him with all my heart.

One thing God made me realize during this time was that He gives us, to some extent, free will, which means, for now, that He allows people to do wrong things. And, sometimes those things are done to those of us who are His children. We can grumble and complain when it happens—making it harder on ourselves—or we can choose to continue trusting him. Hallelujah! Thank you, God, for teaching me to trust in you always and in all circumstances. Am I perfect at this? No, I am not, but as the Bible says, "I press toward the mark."

Chapter 23

Some people blame Daddy for leaving everything to Ruth and not making sure it would be left to Bill and me. I do not blame him, because I understand why he did it. After Vickie was killed, Ruth said she would have no one if Daddy preceded her in death. Daddy told me this when he was in the hospital, several years after Vickie's death. She convinced him she might need whatever money there was to assure her care in later years. This was when they made new wills, both alike, designating Bill and me as primary heirs after both their deaths.

Daddy trusted Ruth. If you cannot trust your spouse, who can you trust? He would never have believed she would lie to him and that she would change her will.

Someone had said he should have set up a trust. But Ruth would never have agreed to that, even if it had occurred to Daddy. Daddy did what any spouse should do, in my opinion. He did what he could to please his spouse; to assure that she was taken care of, never thinking that she would betray him and treat Bill and me in such a way.

I cannot tell you that I blame Ruth for wanting the will to be that way. I think I might have wanted the same thing if I were her. However, breaking her word and changing her will afterward is a different story and was wrong. I believe the nieces she left the money and house to were just as wrong in taking it as Ruth was in giving it to them. They knew it should have come to Bill and me. It was rightfully ours, but they chose to take it anyway. In spite of this, God gave the ability to forgive.

Chapter 24

During the trial of the young man who killed Vickie, I had sat in the courtroom looking at him, his mother and sisters. I thought that as awful as this was for us, it had to be worse for his family. I realized I would rather be sitting where we were than where they were; that it was better to suffer having a loved one killed than having a loved one who did the killing. It seems that would have been unbearable. And God brought that to mind when our inheritance was taken from us. I thought about those who took it. I realized I would rather be in my shoes than theirs. I would rather be the one it was taken from than the one who took it from someone else.

What God did during this time and the way He carried us was worth much more than any amount of money. I was amazed that that neither Bill nor I was really angry. Oh, there was briefly some initial anger when we first learned the contents of the will, which God readily took away. I assure you, on our own we would have been raging. But, God certainly "calmed the sea," and the anger was just not there. Oh, we did not like what was done; we still do not because it was wrong. But we were not ranting and raving about it. Instead, I was praying for God to let us be in that situation just what He would have us be.

I was so hurt, but God also took the pain. Think about losing that much money—and if you can even imagine what it would be like, you'll understand when I say, "It hurt." I asked God to take away the hurt, and, praise His Holy Name, He did. Oh, I must tell you it still hurt some, but not that deep pain. He taught me to turn my mind from the money and thank Him for all the blessings we have. I still have to do that occasionally, when something I see or hear brings it back to mind. I have to turn my mind, my thoughts to the Lord and His goodness, rather than dwell on what has happened. He taught me to "set my mind on things above and not on this earth" (Colossians 2:10).

Chapter 25

I thank Him that He has given me the grace to forgive, and I know only He can do that. Pleasing Him is much, much more important than any amount of money. Knowing Jesus Christ made such a difference in and through these experiences. In Him, I am free from hate, self-pity, and the list could go on and on. No, I have not arrived. I still experience all those emotions, and sometimes I am sorry to say I still fall prey to them. But, as I look to Him for cleansing, I'm free to enjoy my relationship with Him. I am free to enjoy the abundant life He came to give when He said, "I am come that they might have life and they might have it more abundantly" (John 10:10).

Matthew 6:19 says, "Lay not up for yourselves treasures on earth, where moth and rust doth corrupt. But lay up for yourselves treasures in heaven, where neither moth nor rust doth corrupt, and where thieves do not break through and steal; for where your treasure is, there will your heart be also." That's all that truly has meaning. And Bill and I knew that someday, God would make all things right. The Bible also tells us in Romans 12:20, "If your enemy is hungry, feed him; If he is thirsty, give him a drink; For in so doing you will heap coals of fire on his head" (NKJV). I'm not sure exactly what that means—heaping coals of fire on their head—but Bill and I most surely heaped coals of fire on Ruth's head.

God gave me (or us) the grace to be kind and good to her all these years. And, apparently, she was our enemy. A true friend could not do to someone what she did to us. But God has taught me that I am not responsible for how another person treats me or what they do to me. I'm responsible before Him for how I treat them.

Finally, God, through the power of the Holy Spirit, gave me the grace to forgive her again, and also her nieces. It does not mean what they did was right, because it wasn't. It doesn't mean I like what they did; I don't. It simply means I will obey Him when He says in His Word: "Recompense to no men evil for evil." God also gave me the grace to pray for them: "Pray for those who despitefully use you."

Chapter 26

I received this from a friend, Bonnie, whom I had asked to pray for us and with whom I shared during this time. She said:

> "It is good and heartwarming to know friends like you, Bobbie....folks who can TRULY forgive and go forward. Lots of us will try and I mean try hard. Some of us just don't quite get to that step, but we keep on trying. Although some might feel that you and Bill got nothing, I see that both or you received MUCH MORE than her estate, something far more valuable than money or land, something more lasting... things called LOVE, understanding, decency, and a CLEAR understanding of God and what HE considers 'treasures of this earth.'"

Also, during that time, I received this quote (can't remember exactly how it came to me, but it had/has great meaning):

> "Ordinary riches can be stolen, real riches cannot. In your soul are infinitely precious things that cannot be taken from you." – Oscar Wilde

Chapter 27

Below is something I wrote sometime after discovering Ruth had changed her will. It was actually prompted by someone asking, "What is your idea of a wealthy person?" This is what I believe God gave me in response to the question.

What is your idea of a wealthy person? What really constitutes true wealth? What a person achieves in a career, a bank account or investments may be one type of wealth or success. We look at their positions in business, the houses they live in, the cars they drive, etc. That is true wealth in the worldly sense. This type of wealth is often temporary. It can be lost during a poor economy—recession—bad investments, or simply through death. The Bible says in 1 Timothy 6:7, "For we brought nothing into this world, and it is certain we can carry nothing out." There is another type of wealth that can never be taken away, and it comes from having a relationship with Jesus Christ. A successful or wealthy person is one who has truly learned to love, to laugh, to give of themselves, and in doing so, to truly live. It is one who, regardless of circumstances, can give a smile to another person or offer a helping hand to someone in need.

In 1 John 3:17, the Bible asks: Where is the compassion or the love of God if we see a brother or sister in need, and we do not give them those things? But a wealthy person has

Chapter 27

learned to respond to the needs God puts in front of him, whether it be physical help or financial, whatever the need is. He gave us an example of that in Luke 10:30-37 about the Good Samaritan, who responded to a need of someone he didn't even know.

A wealthy person is one who can overcome in difficult circumstances, rather than being overcome. He has learned to persevere, to endure. He has learned, as Philippians 4:13 says: "I can do all things through Christ Who strengthens me." He believes God when He said in Hebrews 13:5, "I will never leave you nor forsake you." He is strengthened by His Spirit in the inner man. He has learned, "God is our refuge and strength; a very present help in trouble" (Psalm 46:1).

A wealthy person is one who can put self aside to serve God and their fellow man; one who has learned from Philippians 2:4 to "Look not only on his own things, but also on the things of others," and who has learned to truly care about others.

A wealthy person is one who has learned acceptance of things that cannot be changed. He can go on and do his best in any situation. He is one who leaves the injustices of some people and the injustices of this world to his heavenly Father. He has learned to forgive as he has been forgiven. He has learned to treat others well, regardless of how he is treated. He has learned to extend the same grace to others that has been extended to him in and through Jesus Christ. He is a person who gives himself to God, to His plans and purposes, and then to others, serving God and others in agape love, through the power of the Holy Spirit.

A wealthy person is one who has learned from 1 Corinthians 13 that if one does not have love (agape love, which is love in actions), one is nothing. The wealthy person has learned that love suffers long. (This reminds me of 2 Peter 3:9 where God's Word tells us He is long-suffering—not willing that any should perish, but that all should come to repentance). A wealthy person has learned that love is kind, not easily provoked; that love seeks not its own, bears and endures all things, rejoices in the truth, and even more stated in 1 Corinthians 13. They have learned the more you give love away, the more you have. It is an inexhaustible supply from the Lord.

To sum it up, the wealthiest people are not necessarily the ones with the most money. Instead, they are those who know God through Jesus Christ; those who have received the Spirit of adoption, whereby we cry, "Abba, Father"; with the Spirit Himself bearing witness with our spirit, that we are the children of God; and, if children, "then joint heirs with Christ". Their treasures are not here on this earth, but in heaven. Now they may have earthly treasure or riches here, but they know their real treasure is in heaven. That's where their hearts are. They are seeking first the kingdom of God and His righteousness. They have "set their affections on things above and not on this earth." They have "put on tender mercies, kindness, humbleness of mind, meekness, longsuffering; forgiveness."

They have learned to "forgive even as God, for Christ's sake has forgiven us." And above all, they have "put on love, which is the bond of perfectness."

The peace of God rules in their hearts and minds. They walk in praise, worship, and obedience to God—the God who gave His Son, Jesus Christ, to pay the penalty for our sin. They know the "height, depth and width of God's love," and rest in His assurance that nothing can ever separate them from that love.

They have truly learned to live life at its best and at its fullest. It is indeed an abundant life, filled with love for God and others. It is a life filled with joy and the peace of God that passes all understanding. They have learned that there are riches much more important than all the money in the world or the greatest position they could have. They are the riches of the heart and spirit—riches made possible only through the Lord Jesus Christ. In Him, they live and move and have their being.

The Bible says, "eye has not seen, nor ear heard; neither has entered into the heart of man the things which God has prepared for them that love Him" (1 Corinthians 2:9). These wealthy people, as did Abraham, are looking for a city whose maker and builder is God.

For those who are discovering these riches, or are on the journey of that discovery, thank God for His unspeakable gift, for His love, His mercy, His grace; and for all He has given us in and through Jesus Christ.

Chapter 28

I stated earlier I would tell you something more about my mother. About ten years after Daddy left home, Mother met a widower, Johnny Jenkins. They began seeing each other and eventually married. Johnny was also a Christian and a blessing to our family. They had twenty years together before Johnny's death. He was so loved by all the family.

Mother forgave Daddy and Ruth, even though Ruth never asked or apologized. Did she like what they did? No. But we are commanded to forgive others as we have been forgiven. And so, Mother was obedient in forgiving them.

If you asked me who in this world comes the nearest to loving me like Jesus, I would tell you it was her. Mother loved me unconditionally. I do not think there is anything I could do that would cause her to stop loving me. I know there have been times when she was displeased with my actions. In fact, when I was a kid, sometimes that displeasure was directed toward a certain part of my body! But, regardless of my behavior, her love for me was constant. She taught me unselfishness, kindness, and many other things. And she taught me to love others, more by the way she lived than words. She loved in and by her actions. When she was treated badly, she continued to treat others well. Oh, she may have been angry at first, but in the end, she always returned good to whoever was involved.

When the good she did was unappreciated, that, too, did not stop her. She simply continued to serve. This was also a lesson in humility. You have to humble yourself to continue to do good to people when it is not appreciated or when they mistreat you. Human nature wants to respond in like manner, but my mother chose not to do so.

I have never known her to seek revenge against another person. Her life has been just the opposite. She gave of herself sacrificially and financially, when she could. I have seen her give financially when it meant she would do without. She never looked for nor expected anything in return. Her motive was not reciprocation; her motive was love for another person.

These and many other things are why I say she comes the closest to loving me like Jesus. No, I'm not saying she loves exactly like Jesus. None of us can do that. But we strive toward that goal. Jesus/God loves us unconditionally. The Bible tells us in Romans 8:38-39 that nothing can separate us from his love. He loves us, not because of who we are, but because of who He is, and He is love. He loved us while we were still sinners; separated from God the Father by that sin. Jesus gave himself for us before we asked. He forgave us before we asked. We received the love and forgiveness bestowed upon us by believing in Him and turning from our sin and unbelief. How blessed we are to be so loved. And, how blessed I was in the mother God gave me!

Chapter 29

I don't know what is or will be going on in the lives of whoever may read this. But whatever it is — a walk with Jesus (Praise), or a walk of unbelief and/or disobedience (Prayer), but may we always seek God and His will above our own. He wants only the best for us. He and His way are the very best. He says He came that we might have life and have it more abundantly, and that life is found only in Him; faith in His Son, Jesus Christ; and our walk with Him. For any who are not His children, you can trust Him. You can trust the one who hung on a cross, shedding His blood and paying the penalty for your sin and mine. You can trust the One Who sent Him; the One Who loved us so much that He gave His only begotten son. No one will ever love us as much as God/Jesus.

John 3:16 "For God so loved the world that He gave His only begotten Son, that whosoever believes in Him should not perish, but have everlasting life."

www.ingramcontent.com/pod-product-compliance
Lightning Source LLC
Chambersburg PA
CBHW060343080526
44584CB00013B/896